Maxine's
NIGHT BEFORE CHRISTMAS

Illustrated by John Wagner
Written by Bill Gray

Published in the United States of America
by Hallmark Cards, Inc.

ISBN: 0-87529-703-X

PRINTED IN CHINA.

My support hose were hung
By the chimney with care.
(I hung them last Christmas
And just left them there.)

After watching the cat rip
The presents to shreds.

And I in my long johns
And ratty night cap
Had just settled my butt
For a long winter's nap.

When out on the lawn
There arose such a clatter,
I swore at the window,
"What the (blank) is the matter?"

I tore open the window,
Not a second to tarry,
All ready to throw
The noisemaker a berry.

A bright moon was lighting
 The new-fallen snow...
And I had a moon of my own
Set to show.

Floyd was beside me,
Paw pointing the way
Toward eight tiny reindeer
Hitched up to a sleigh...

And a little old driver
So cheery and quick,
I thought for a moment
That I would be sick.

Like a bat out of...you know,
His reindeer they came,
And I whistled and shouted
And called them some names--
"Hey, Hornhead! Hey, Furface!
Hey, Weiner and Turkey!
Yo, Klutzy and Mangy
And Venison Jerky!

Stay off of my porch!
Get away from my wall!
Now hit the road, hit the road,
Hit the road, all!"

But as pedestrians before
 My old Buick, they fly
And head for high ground
With great fear in their eyes,
So up to my rooftop
The fleabags they flew,
With a sleigh full of toys
And old Fruitcake-Breath, too.

As I reached for my slingshot
And a marble as well,
Down the chimney St. Nicholas
Tumbled and fell.

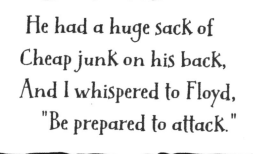

He had a huge sack of
Cheap junk on his back,
And I whispered to Floyd,
"Be prepared to attack."

His eyes, they were squinting,
His toy bag was draggin',
And I felt for a moment
Like I'd soon be gaggin'.

He was dressed all in red,
With a bell on his hat,
And a belt of black leather
To hold back the fat.

He had a broad face
And a little round belly
That shook when I nailed him
With a handful of jelly.

He was chubby and plump,
Well, actually, porky,
And I laughed when I tripped him
(He looked pretty dorky).

He was like a beached whale,
Unable to budge,
And he tasted good, too,
If the dog was a judge.

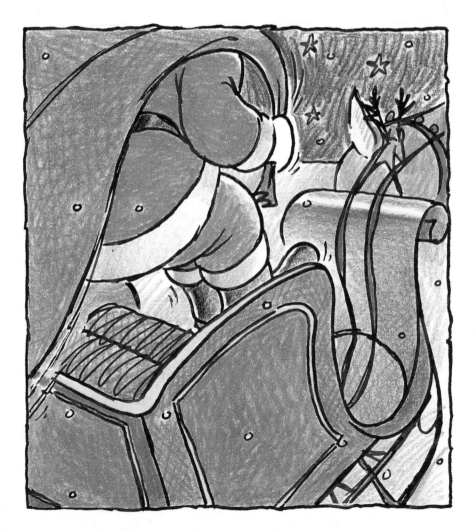

A big bag of jerky
Turned Floyd mighty chipper,
While for me was a pair
Of brand-new bunny slippers.